GW01606155

TOTAL RECALL

TOTAL RECALL

Poems by

Colin Rowbotham

LITTLEWOOD PRESS

5 Slater Bank
Hebden Bridge
West Yorkshire HX7 7DY

for Sidney Briskin

Published by Littlewood Press
Printed at the Arc & Throstle Press, Todmorden, Lancs
Typeset by Bryan Williamson, Manchester

ISBN 0 946407 33 9

Acknowledgements are due to: *Arvon Competition 1985 Anthology, The Green Book, Kites, Louth Festival Anthology, The North, Poetry Nottingham, Seven Years On* and *Touchstones 5*. 'The Family Late Summer' won 1st Prize in the Lake Aske Memorial Competition 1984 and 'Ken' won 1st Prize in The Old Bull Poetry Competition (Barnet) 1985.

CONTENTS

THE CHRISTENING GIFTS

Who'll give him the smile?
I, said the Grandad.
To wise eyes and easy mouth
I'll add a glad hand
That seems without guile.

Mine the will to endure
And the way to hurt, stated
The Grandmother. Sure-
Cutting tongue, iron spine
Are all mine.

My touch like the sun
On his shoulders, a mesh
To hold others
When older
Said Mother.

The tunnels of mind,
Muttered Father,
My patience
And anger to light them, the rhythm
Of words to delight him.

I'll be the peg, cried self: a
Small but constant something else
Beneath these cloaks you hang on me,
I'll take
The strain until I break.

FLOWERS AND THORNS

When Dad and Mother went away
To talk out whether they should stay
Together, friends took John and me
Off somewhere for the day.

Was it the summer of the year
That I turned ten? A Saturday
Or Sunday? Strange that details blur
When feelings stay so clear.

Beneath the hot blue day: a heath
Yellow with gorse. Between us both:
Untold anxiety – instead
We played at hide-and-seek

All afternoon. I learned that gorse
Is good to hide inside; the thorns
Won't hurt if they're ignored. Of course,
I won the game. I knew

(As kids do) that to win would save
The day somehow. My parents stayed
Together. Gain and loss were too
Entangled to undo.

MOONFALL

I never saw you in your prime,
Skymother. A woman of substance
Then, they say; as dense and lucid
As a split flint. Chief mover
At festivities; a guide
To townless folk moonlighting
Across cat-striped sands.

I glimpsed you late last night
As we drove from a party
Where no-one spoke your name. You'd paled
And lost weight (did iron
Sap your magic?) The car swung
In lane and you dropped like an eggshell behind
The massed cartons and brandnames of town.

HOME TIME

Crudely lopped blackpoplars, leant
In line against a winter sky
As bright and dented as a strip
Of hammered tin.

Schoolboys clip the sharp
Corner past the navy, scissored spire
Of Birch Church, trashing leafmounds in a rush
To make the buses; rank impatient engines
Bantering to be off.

Four o'clock. A last keen
Shard from day's bleak end, embedded
Solid in that rutted, muddy lane:
Myself – twelve thirteen fourteen – blown along
And running with the rest.

POLE HILL

An obelisk stands on a hill
Near Chingford. I discovered this
When I and my small daughter
Had some time to kill.

A metal notice, overlaid
With drab, official paint, proclaims
That longitude from Greenwich
Once ran through its base

But now has shifted nineteen feet.
I bumped the pushchair to the east,
We wheeled and squinted northwards
Through grey rags of sleet.

Perhaps the silly Toytown name
Of Chingford prompted me to say:
"Why don't we do a journey
Round the world today?"

I saw a road that, from my sad
Childhood suburb, leapt and spanned
The dirty Mersey, swept into
Another land

Existing only in the mind,
Not elsewhere – like this zero line
Which mostly ghosts its furrow
Through sand, sea and ice.

"We'd make it back for teatime, love."
My child was not amused. We shoved
Off, down to where her mother
Would be missing us.

ENIGMA

Sometimes, when evening autumn winds
Besieged my childhood house, I'd almost see
A motley figure, brown and green;
Capering corkscrews with the leaves.

Night brewed stronger ghosts: grey suits
Semaphored at doors; the long
Norseman, bone knife ready, nudged,
Slow as a looming ice-cap, to my bed.

But such things were phantoms, shot
Like photons from a brainbox overpowered
By fright or fever – Mother, day,
A drench of bedside light would see them off.

It was otherwise that wet
Manchester day, when Mother trailed
Brother and me through acres of glum,
Echoing museum galleries.

Rank on rank of carved sarcophagi,
Belying with secretive, bland smiles
The withered things inside, gave way
To a plain, grey box. She raised the lid, we saw

A naked man on his side, smooth skin
Dewed with cold sweat, his blue eyes open wide
But unmoving. I, tiptoeing to view him, said:
"Is he dead?" "Yes," she replied.

Years later I went back. He was gone,
As I knew he would be. Though my dreams
Now are rich and hard to recollect, he lies
Inside my skull, unshifted by the days.

LOST CONNECTION

for my Grandfather and unborn child

I

Some calls you can't forget: her face
lit, batting upwards from the phone
the news that, after five years,
we'd conceived.

Another: the way shock locked
my mother's grip around the handset; grief
invading her voice so fast
I knew he'd died.

We'd not long since
visited him: old
soldier in the Chelsea Hospital,
brewing us a cup of tea. He spoke

In a slow Mancunian roll –
cigar smoke against dark
oak-panelling, a bass oboe. Spoke
like a man who took

Pains even with trifles; from
the sly courting of our small
adopted daughter, to that look –
pouched eyelids winking, lip long-drawn –

When I pulled his surprise fiver out
of my overcoat. "If you don't mind,
I won't come to the gate; it's turned
a bit chilly." Our goodbyes

And Christmas wishes. When we had
our unexpected news, she said:
"If it's a boy, let's call
it after him." He would have been so glad.

II

An army cemetery, stuck miles
outside London. January had turned too cold
for tears to run freely. Snow
frosting our toecaps. My aside

To both brothers: "Like a clip
from a John le Carré film." Black
backing of cypress, the taped strains
of his regiment's march: *The British Grenadiers*.

No wreaths by request. Mother, whose coat
looked too large for her, wordlessly tossed
carnations into his grave. My turn
came; I threw our three and wished

I'd one more for the unborn child
replacing him in a sort
of Changing of the Guard: his death
at the old year's end, its growing with the new.

III

Some calls you can't forget: my voice
listing symptoms coldly, then
a sudden plea "– how soon
can the doctor come?"

Hands held in silence. I'd tried
to cheer her earlier; she knew
she was losing the child. Our toddler's toys
still cluttered the bed; an alarm clock

Showed the wrong time. The locum came
within the hour, unsmiling man
who told her *relax*. I was out of the room
when she yelled to be sick – barged in to find

Her blacking-out, skin pale and grained
as a paper towel. "She is all right,"
he stated, phoned an ambulance
and slunk off like an unapplauded turn.

IV

She told me later of the high
hospital couch; the grave, alert
doctor's face eclipsing the light
as he wordlessly prodded – then

Pulled on a rubber glove, stuck
a scissored scoop inside her and hauled
out a reddened blob of flesh
untouched by human hand.

One and three-quarter inches long –
the pictures in the books she'd read
had shown it in clean detail. "Anything
to see?" she ventured. "Nothing to see," he said.

That was all she saw of it. It went
onto a trolley to be wheeled
away. A shrimp in a plastic bag,
like the end of a takeaway meal.

V

"The end of an era," one brother said
when Grandad went. The old man saw
a Depression and the two world wars
that bracketed it. I think they'd been

The high spots of his life. He lived
for the army and died in it. Eighty four
years; a long and punishing run
with an easy end. Our child had known

Eleven weeks inside the womb;
grown fingers and toes, but couldn't keep
its hold on life. The links are gone
and I must forge connections where I can.

THE FAMILY LATE SUMMER

We none of us sleep well. Small
Dot coughs from her cot; across the hall,
At the last train's passing, Gran's glass
Of dentures chatters, eating the heart
Out of her dreams.
In his bunk the boy
Strips thin blankets away, strokes the cool wall.
Your snores increase, to cease as you budge
Me to bed's edge. We are all
Stuck with unease, a set
Of sweat-basted chickens, turning
In a dark, uncaring kitchen.

What cooks? We can't detect
Recipe or pattern in the quick
Retreat of footsteps after smashed
Glass against concrete, the seesaw
Of sirens, shrilling whistles, drunken street
Altercations that escalate.
Each in our turn we lie awake
And yearn for a break in the hot, sullen
Animal weather.

It hasn't come by breakfast. Gran sits
Knitting, unravelling, pecking dry toast.
The boy moons about, Dot squalls
For more, you frown at bills, and I hear
The radio rabbitting stocks, shares
And everyday atrocities.

Has it begun to mimic
My thoughts? I'm no longer sure
Which way the tape unwinds. I'd dream
If I could take the consequences – I wish
I could stand at the window and watch white
Lightning flashes dealing blue
Shadows about the courtyard; blank
Out as the sky splits
With a racket like a brickbat-crapping ogre;
Wake later, safe
In bed, to see you at the open window,
Holding conversation with the rain.

ALPHABEAST

Five, I must have been, trailing him
At school through a thicket of print
Down that long afternoon.
No sign in thorned confusion. I raised
My head, Miss said: "You're not trying," I returned
To the grey pages – without warning
He roared out at me, a revealed beast
From a trick picture (can you find our friend
Amid the jungle?) *I'd* both hands full
With clinging to his tail.

We cleared, in one elated leap,
Tracts of desolation – graded
Readers flickered past us
Like coloured milestones – were gone. I glimpsed
Idiotic toytowns, knocked shocked, skittle-stiff
Policemen toppling; then we were on
To a bigger world, where moon and sun
Came closer, and his purring filled my ears
Always. My skull vaulted island seas.
His tongue was my pillow.

Worlds within words. I grew and learned
To come, as I grew, at his call.
I came ashamed that no
Photo conjured partner taste or place
Like his print on well-thumbed white. He became quite
The ogre, cheapening other worlds
Unfairly with his. I couldn't speak
To outsiders; woke up locked in a tall
Glass-walled tower. Although I chattered
It was only from cold.

How do you unlearn words, return
Them to innocent shapes? I tried
Staring him dumb and saw,
More and more, his features mirrored back
At mine from the glass, saw then it would take death
Or madness to split us; paced the length
Of my cage, coming to terms with new
Strength and old weaknesses, ventured a look
At worlds beyond walls, decided *yes*
And sprang towards the glass.

MEMORIES?

Scraps from the wordless age fall
White from a bleak skyslate, framed
By what must have been pram – huge hands
On the worldrim hoist him,
Bumping through hubbub, steam – doors slam
To reopen on two stockinged legs receding
Along a landing. With such snippets
Precious as old manuscripts, who needs
To know if they are faked?

OLD STORY

Old stories reproduce themselves
Without quite duplicating.

High summer noon:
When a matchflame is invisible
And a toppled cup of coffee infiltrates
Baked roadside earth in seconds,
Leaving only grounds.
When something aloof and massive sounds
To be humming to itself
Below the horizon, and overhead
A few birds preen on glinting strands of wire.

A single puff of wind, which shook
Slender, heavy-headed stems of grass,
Lifted his hair and stirred him to his feet.
He sneered at his folks, reposing
In post-picnic sloth, and took a stroll
Down the deserted road.

From a stile in the hedgerow gap,
He could see, two parched fallow fields away,
A dense copse, hunched in hedgehog silhouette
Against the peerless, taut blue sky.

Dad and Mother said you shouldn't
Go in woods alone. He stood,
Munched the pros and cons a bit,
And brushed into the thicket. It was cool.

The path wound on for such a small
Wood; and once a scuttling thing
Hid in dead leaves – but no sunless shapes
Swung from the trees. The path gave out
In a sunlit spot, in which he sat and dreamed
For most of an afternoon.

The world was a forest: valleys and hills were sheathed
In an endless switchback stretch
Of sculpted turquoise. There was rich
Variety of life.

It was cold when he woke. A single field
Of barley blew to the rim of sight.
No trees. Some way away, two strangers
Ran towards him, shouting in the wind.

SIGHTINGS

An oak-tree, green and sodden, seen
Through rain-distorted glass one long
Gone joyless morning as I sat
Crammed in, in infant school – I'd been
Botching away at sums, but when
(Knowing the answers must be wrong)
I turned to the tree, it stood and met
My beggar's look with silence – then
The memory surfaced, hot and strong

Of fever shaking me from sleep.
How, listening to the road of all-
Night lorries from the Menai Bridge,
I'd watched their splaying headlights sweep,
Diagonalwise, the ceiling, slide
To nowhere down the bedroom wall,
Then slice again past curtain's edge
And so on. It had kept me wide-
Awake for hours, that steady crawl.

No easy getaways from pain
Then. That was clear enough. But why
That roll of lorries? Once around
The corner – what? Once, down the lane
With Grandpa, toddling after tea,
He'd stooped to hold me very high
Against the hedge. His speckled hand
Bent blackthorn back to let me see
Four dunnock's eggs, blue as the sky

That June. Now rain. I sat and dreamed
In the rain through years of lessons, yearned
For times to match that blue again.
At fifteen, on a beach, I seemed
To have glimpsed it. No, not quite; the tone
Too strident, like the sand that burned
My feet, the brazen sun, the din
Of trippers. Needing to be alone
(Poor thing) I shrugged my shoulders, turned

Towards the bay. Two islands stood
Blue on the skyline; hazy, locked
In distant mystery. Seen close-
Up from a dinghy: not so good.
Just lumps of rock. Among the dunes
Where urgent pairs of lovers mocked
My own desires, I turned my face
Away as radios played tunes
For aching teenage hearts that cocked

Lust in my swimtrunks. I unlocked
The caravan door and brushed inside.
Dark petals bloomed before my eyes,
Then withered= In the mirror, pocked
And silvery with age, full-length
I stood. And who was I? I tried
To answer, but to my surprise,
I knew. And laughed with sudden strength.
The oak-tree had at last replied.

TIME TRAINS

3.03

The clock ticked, the child turned
to the window game again. Behind
rain-rusting railings, tall, blueshaven
men (unlike his father) passed
the window (men without
moustaches) striding past
the windowframe, they vanished. Rain
twisted the glass beneath his hand;
he gazed
into the basement area where
the rain struck green-smeared flagstones
by a bricked-up doorway;
silver, bouncing rain,
leaching the light out of the afternoon.

3.15

The clock chimed quarter-past,
the child turned
in from the window to observe
the vaunting man astride a rearing horse
atop the clock;
his right hand grasping
space a spear should
have filled.
Two weeping women pled
at his side; all four in ormolu.
The child,
clenching his fist as tightly as
he could,
could still feel space inside.

3.49

The clock, changing
its pace,
raced, the child turned
the roughened-edged pages of a book
of nursery rhymes; grim, gaunt and gaudy
beggars stalked, grotesque and brazen
beneath the pale stare of a someone
high
behind a diamond-pane; "Hark hark!
the dogs do bark," he read

aloud from memory and then,
realising who had spoken,
added:
"I am three."

4.00

The clock struck four,
the child knelt down
on the floor and turned
the thick key of his clockwork engine; let
it slide out of his hand along
slick rails, turning, watched it
wind away towards the fading,
painted hills on the far wall, hit
a kink
returning,
fall, wheels churning noisily,
on its side until
the whirringblueblackshiningspring
ran down.

0.00

All day the clock ran on, at night
it gave out; the child turned
in bed; in dreamtime turned
a roundabout where vaunting beggars
waved from their clockwork steeds
to the figure
of a child who clanged a brazen bell;
who, pellmell, burst his racing train
through the bricked-up mouth of a greensmeared tunnel,
called – dwindling to a farbluehaven –
to a tall, drawn man (unlike his
father) behind a veil of rain,
who, with his free hand as the other wrote,
was wave wave waving
goodbye.

MISSING LOCKS

My dad kept keys
In an oblong, round-cornered
Tobacco tin when I was young:
Flat, dullyellow Yales.
A butterfly wind-up one, tiny gunbarrels
For bureaus and watches,
A rust-roughened, jigsaw-toothed
Giant from someone's backdoor.
      Not ours;
Though I probed all the locks
That I knew of,
They never did yield.
      Yet, fingering that metal nest
Gave pleasure – very like the sort
I get these days
From memories, letters,
Words.

GRANNY AND GRANDPA STRULDBRUGS'

The right time to visit? As soon
As it's finished raining, when
You're eight years of age, on a late afternoon
In autumn if possible. Take
The pocked gravel path that curves
Past shivering evergreen shrubs to the black
Battery of windows, twist the knob
On the unlocked door. You're back

In the hall once again, and all's
As it always was: the same
Sombre clan of portraits masking the walls
With obsolete postures, the squat
Knick-knack stocked whatnot, the clock
Above the barometer. *No change*, though you
Try tapping the glass, it's been done
As if to frustrate you. Through

The chink of a doorway come low
Mumbles, dittoed by the neat
Pinking of china teacups; all of the slow
Motions of a meal consumed
Over twenty-thousand times,
Multiplied by thirty-two chews, multiplied
By how many toothless mouthfuls . . .
Oughtn't you to go inside?

Say hello and look at the floor,
Teasing the carpet patterns
Into faces, while your own reddens, unsure
Of how to continue from there?
They can't provide a beginning,
Perhaps they've forgotten; it's just like a game
Where no-one knows the rules – do they
Even remember your name?

You could have died, and wished *they* would,
On such occasions; but now
That you need to talk, it isn't any good
Trying to hold a conversation
With the shapes in your head. How
Truly Swift wrote about Struldbrugs; they become
Disordered as the years go by
And irrevocably dumb.

TO MAGGIE

Five Augusts back we set up house
Then married. If that sounds
Like a story's opening, it felt then
The happiest of endings; one to halt
The film in its tracks, sealing protagonists
For good in amber sunset.

Suns go under – and what's amber?
A token blink, splitting
Go from *stop*; and yet the way in which
You've braced this household on its bed of love
Embodies such skill that I expect the walls
To obstruct time's thoroughfare.

No: the flow pulls homes along
With all else. Though their bright
Promises look to be fixed; like twin
Sunlit glitterings on an iron track,
Apparently static, they skim and the lines
Soon approach a conclusion.

I daren't trust we'll meet up in some
Infinity, yet hope
The light we mirrored in this house shines
On still, when all of our hulls have been swept
Out into tracklessness; bobbing, bobbinning
Till the sea folds them under.

HOMECOMING

Wind noses the tentflap like a great
Blind watchdog. Wife and child
Breathe gently in sleep. I inhale
A last cigarette. My sense of smell
Though under-used, abused, can still recall
More keenly than the other four. Sharp sap
From camp-trampled grass, the sweet
Insinuating scent of butane, blend
To cheat time, draw other, long-neglected
Absent odours to this site.

Blankets at Scoutcamp; their motherly smell
Of lanolin, twinned with a clinical
Disinfectant reek that evoked cold
Stethoscope on chest, sly games
Of doctor/nurse with girls. When folded
Rightly, blankets showed red L's –
For love or lust? Coarse, jeering tales
Of what males did together passed
From mouth to ear in the dark; remained,
Despite ashamed desire, only talk.

Hungry for touch, I fed
Instead on other senses; wind-
Blown words of morning prayer, so slight
In the open air; the cloying ooze
Of condensed milk on my tongue; peered
Choking through woodsmoke aroma,
At shadow-rags and flames that chased
My mind through mazes; gorged and stupefied
Self into a state where I was near
Impossible to touch.

And until last night I never made
Love on a hard tent-floor, or heard
The loved one's urgent whispers blend
With endless river palaver. Later, soft
Ghostvoices from the years contrived
A dream where I wandered calm; apart
Yet a part of things. Tonight the wind
And rain assail this flimsy home. Let's hope
The guyropes hold. I nestle, turn
To hug my sleeping wife.

TOKENS

Childhood on Sunday; TV screens
Leaden and rainy as the sky
Outside. We'd play Monopoly
To chase away the greyness – vivid, striped
Oblongs in a dish of yellow light.

Winning was nice, but trappings held
Much more attraction than the rules:
Chunky wood houses and hotels
In green and red, flash banknotes and those two
Heavy, metal tokens: hat and boot.

I couldn't bring myself to start
Down Old Kent Road by ship – or worst
Of all, that stiff, grim racing-car.
Tophat had dash, but boot, each tiny crease,
Welt and lacehole perfect, was the best.

Thus shod, I'd pound the pavements; make
Outlandish bids because I liked
A placename; take the waterworks
As fair exchange for Mayfair; win by luck . . .
Sometimes. Haven't really changed that much.

LIT UP

Magical mostly – those first tastes:
Alcohol, tobacco, the long list
Of circumscribed chemicals ingested
Years back. My heart a huge
Rib-buffeting balloon, released
By its change of pace as tongue perused
The seam of gums and teeth for that initial
Fugitive tingle.

Spells, my dad called them: long wands
Of newspaper, kinked at the tip
Like a wizard's cap. A xylophone plink
From scattered kindling, the scratch
And rush of a match – blue and gold-
Skeined, elongating plumes, their hot
Hearts transparent, licked the rim
Of paper, knitting stick to stick.

Disenchantment, as that quick,
Leaping interconnection of dull
Sticks and squarefaced coalblocks turned
Too soon into a uniform
Orange greed that sank to ash.
My own sure-fire illuminations roar
For more also – grow, once kindled,
Into flames not worth the candle.

THE BOY AND PANDORA

The next tread creaks, the clock dictates
in even terms above his head.
The boy has reached the landing, and
ajar, the end-door shows a strip
of sunfaded carpeting, the even
gleam of bedstead rails.

He edges in, untouched
by door or door-jamb; glimpses,
but troubles to ignore
the black oak chest –

Knowing the story
of old; knowing
what sort of box
is better not unlocked.

His own vision of the tale: a huge
stone-furnished, dust-upholstered room,
in which she elects to approach
the single knick-knack
on a marble mantelpiece.

At that moment he
should have walked to the single
small window set high in the wall;
unlatched and swung it out to gaze
on an orchard in May.

But just as she
unlids
the alabaster box, his eye stalks
to the mediaeval print
above that too-made bed:

A chill nativity, where wall-
eyed sneerers, in odd
arthritic attitudes, adore
a mannikin with kaolin-grey skin.

A paper scrap
in the casket reads:
Your lot is this. Then panic leads
her out into a garden by Anonymous:
headstones, nettles, dandelions
run to seed.

His window would only show
a stonemason's yard now. He gropes
to the doorway, unwilling to view
what may choose
to take shape in the bed;

Trips, grasping at bannisters all the way down,
to company in the living-room.

KEN

A colleague said of Ken: "That lad's
Got a hole in his head. Ken sat,
Draped at a table; all of space
Hanging before his features. Hard,
I thought then, to sweep a boy
So utterly away

Heartless, but the man had
A point – I felt it acutely when,
After a swimming lesson, Ken's head
Rose above my cubicle. A noise
I'd not heard anyone make before
Hooted out of his mouth; he laughed and laughed
As he flicked my head with hard licks
Of his towel. The way his face moved said
Something had elbowed into the hole
He kept inside his head.

It toyed with him, impervious
To threat or persuasion, then went;
Leaving again the slack look, the old
Hopeless docility, the hole. I've heard
Since that his mum greets callers at the door
In panties and bra; that he once
Did something nasty to a kid
Round the back of his flats – but that won't fix
The abrupt gap in my wall of facts,
Revealed by the glare of an alien face – I can't
Fill in that hole,
And fear its occupant.

A YEAR AND OTHERS
(1985-1986)

I
September

Why open my year with September?
Memory, prompt as the upstretched hand
Of teacher's favourite, prompts me – school
And all that meant: a sharp, judicial
Break with summer freedoms. Turned
Tutor, I act the child, dismember
Years into terms, watch those initial
Hopes, like the emergent sun
On a maths protractor, cloud and crack:
Kit lost, goals missed and bridges burned
Before they're even reached; the planned
(See timetable) erasure of Romance
As French and Latin bite the chalkdust, slain
By well-aimed tomes. And once again,
My schooldays never done, I'm going back.

Revolving with fresh resolutions,
I cycle to work beneath the stale
Luxuriance of horsechestnut leaves –
Always the first to turn: a golden,
Inward-crimping rim. I might
Have learnt this lesson: crude solutions,
Drink less/more exercise embolden
A week or so, then leave me stuck
In self-denial, unlike the code
Of the Jack-the-Lad I teach. As night
Bloats, I distort his crimes and trail
Lost sleep. September fails, green maces split
To spill sleek chestnut rumps. As kids we'd prize
The conker-crop – today it lies
Crushed in ignored abundance on the road.

II
October

Gulls dazzle round scaffolding; out of the blue
The hottest day of the year
Arrives like a misdirected postcard. Beer-
Glasses nudge on white tabletops; a crew
Of workmen squat the kerb in buff,
Lobster and tan. The month starts well enough.

Then bad news as the skies set grey
As concrete: TOTTENHAM RIOT PC KILLED
The headlines dilate. I shove my way
Through cold to the shops. A banshee whoop
As squadcars pass the pushchair, then a troop
Of men marked POLICE on glossy chestnuts. Thrilled,
My daughter squeals: "*Horsies* – look!" "Yes yes," I say.

Dark before seven. Hulking night
Lays siege to our block of flats. The next
Riot reruns my fantasies. To write
Seems fruitless now. My wife dreams of a ripe,
Emerging horsechestnut, wakes me into sex.

Where Church Street joins High, I overtake a black
Man; enormous in disdain,
Parading through autumn detritus his sign
Of self: a dark coat hooked into the back-
Pocket by Rasta greengoldred;
He trails his blackness, dares the world to tread.

Dark by five. We gird up, descend,
Clocks synchronised, into the narrow, cold
Drain of late autumn. Summer sends
More postcards, each paler than the one
Before it – copied photostats. Its sun
Slouching towards the skyline – like an old
Tramp, October shuffles off to an unmourned end.

III
November

Friday November the first. A line of trees
Half-masking each other in perspective: green
On lemon, on rust. As I cycle past, unease

Wheedles – perhaps at the overlap between
Weekend and start of month, a jangling link.
But then, though breaks are hardly ever clean

November and I are always out of sync.

Friday the eighth. To Clerkenwell Court through rain.
Our daughter's adoption dealt with in the wink

Of an eye, at the judge's nod. A three-year skein
Of red-tape snapped so effortlessly. Though
A paving-slab feels lifted from my brain,

Angst wriggles underneath. Three days ago,
On Paula's third birthday, Maggie smiled and said:
"It's positive; I'm pregnant." Yes, I know

I should be glad – I am – and yet the dread
Of another miscarriage is born as doubt on doubt
Cartwheels in imagination, like the dead

Leaves that a week of wind is combing out
From the treetops. This is the month I danced to the brink
Of madness, before I made a turnabout

Nine years since. Now, each ravening night I drink
More, sleep less. The same disruptive pace
As then – and then, one morning, winter's ink-

Black branches letter the ribboned sky, replace
Autumn's confusion, and my mound of piled
Fears is swept away with the leaves. I trace

A clear network of interconnections, not a wild
Fool's masquerade of motley, begin to face
Facts: a daughter adopted, a wife with child.

IV
December

The Festive rush. Cold iron steps vibrate
In memory: that juddering, long ascent
To the top of the playground slide. No losing face
By a climbdown; though I'd shiver, hesitate
On my perch – till, shoved impatiently, I went
Careening down. December is a place

I revisit every year: a set of keeled
And flaking apparatus, parked on grey
Midwinter tarmac – seesaw, swings, the chute
Clogged with leafscraps sodden as congealed
Cornflakes. A lanky, scissoring midday
Shadow stalks before me as I scoot

To make the roundabout before it wheels
Faster than I can mount. I slither, sick
With effort, across the web, manhandled by
A clutch of skinny kids. The month unreels
Itself with the blurred horizon as we pick
Up caterwauling speed. December sky

Flickers its permutations – untamed wool
Snagged on a glinting chip of sun; a pall
Of gaberdine; a nursery high tea
Of flaked fish on a blue plate – till the pull
Unclamps my fingers from the wheel; I fall,
Giddy, on grit-stung palms and knees, to see

Snow falling from a doughy and impassive
Sky – sinking, rising in perspective, slack
As the third day after Boxing Day. The ride
Done . . . though the roundabout still turns with massive
Snowlike momentum. Chalklines highlight black
Revolving spokes. I dust myself off, stride

Through playground gates to the blank sheet of New Year.

V
January

I smoke the raw Lakeland air – my red-veined eyes
Mirrored by dawn sky – as we fidget, wait
For the eight-o-five to London (running late)
A family group, rehearsing its goodbyes

In silence behind the chitchat. How I detest
These station partings: farewells flung about
Like luggage, in a zig-zag lurch for places;
The mime and mouthing from parental faces
Beyond the window as our train hauls out;
Then a shuddering, slow deflation into rest

While the scenery picks up speed. The tumbled fort
Of Fells dazzles like a model-railway setting
In plaster-of-paris, then slides behind our backs.
Ahead: a stringy mop of nimbus wetting
The nondescript hills that clog my view to port . . .

The Romans knew Janus was a two-faced sort:

A politico deploring past mistakes
Whilst glibly pledging radiant tomorrows.
Today it looks more like rain. As the train makes tracks
For Monday and work, anticipation borrows
Colour – or lack of it – from the landscape: brakes

Of thornwork, ivy-lagged sycamores, a forlorn
Scarecrow in its watery, wrinkling field,
A stretch of etceteras – till sudden rays
Of sunlight flip my mind's prism, and I gaze
At winter's blazon: blue, gold; green revealed
On quickened saplings; collide full-tilt with the corn-

Er called January. Then, though the glimpse is gone
From a window which diagonals of rain
Have started punctuating, I remain:
Turning a corner as the train ploughs on.

VI
February

A rogue month. January days'
Assertions dished by sudden cold, a smack
From a slab-wet mackerel. It plays
This first week like a wild card from the pack

Of fifty-two, does February. I track
My bike through snow: a double line
Of intersecting snakebacks. White on black
On white, the parktrees, spiderfine

As a steel engraving. Snow's design
Stands almost ungraffiti'd. Of Spring's plan,
Coded in wood and earth, no sign
At all. A fortnight on I scan the scan

Of my wife's womb – at first see no more than
A snowy blur of grey and white.
Then words flesh out the foetus which began
Existence that October night

Its mother dreamt of growth despite
The withering year. As days expand, a friend
Dies at last, her seven year fight
In cancer's gripe conducted with a blend

Of nimbleness and courage that transcend
My frequent sneers at what I classed
As her crack-brained attitudes. I can't attend
Her funeral that biting, last

February day. That she surpassed
Me at seeing patterns, I only know
With hindsight, now the chance has passed
To look her in the face and tell her so.

VII
March

Light on the move; that backbone-barking
Lintel of dusk inching up by small
Minutes each day. The blind end wall
Of a pub, gold-glazed by level sun; a high
Ease, as daylight strolls wider bounds, remarking
Brickwork, paving fissures, intricate trees
Like parsley tops against the deepening sky.

Cries nudge my thoughts, like seagulls mewing
On the wind. I scout the flat, to find
A squirming pair of slime-dark, blind
Kittens that bleat brief lives to extinction, quite
Ignored by their labouring mother. Nothing doing
Her posture says. A third is born and dies.
A fourth and fifth. I doubt they'll last the night.

Builders invade our flat. Escaping
To a nearby friend's, we grin and bare
Our teeth politely, well aware
That houseguests, with all their best intentions, tend
To irk. Snatched visits home show matters shaping
Better, in spite of mess and turmoil, cat,
Bathroom, kitchen and kittens on the mend.

Sky on the boil: a coloured muddle
Jigsawed by trees; a gate banged back
To smash; whiteorangepurple wrack
Of crocuses; resurrected dead leaves, sailed
Through flexing light; clouds scudding in a puddle . . .
Mutating elements. I think of Jen,
Who died last month when cancer nailed

Her finally – or not? The temple rending –
Then? In our remade home we celebrate,
In silence, Good Friday's tragicomic ending.

VIII
April

"Hey, lookathat: a rocket!" sharp-eyed school
Playmates would urge. Invariably, I –
An easy kid to kid – gawped up through specs,
My infant thirst for prodigies quenched by
A vacant grey and hoots of: "April Fool!"

Now – *plus ça change* – we choose to light the last
Coal fire of winter on All Fool's Day, just
Before the spring's postponed; trudge from our first,
Sleet-spattered Hyde Park picnic to a bust
Front door and drawerfuls of belongings cast

About our newly-ordered flat. Just kids
The police say. Those I teach perhaps, who joke
At simple quarter-truths one had to learn
In earnest. Just a giggle . . . then I choke
Anger with angst . . . the world is on the skids.

A fractured view that fits in with each chunk
Of ugly news. F-one-elevens attack
Libya – confuting all those anodyne
Forecasts. Qadhafi's icon, on a stack
Of papers, fuels my heartbeat. Like some drunk,

See-sawed by an unstable paving stone,
I catch my breath. While others venture weak
Cracks about bombs beneath the muttering beat
Of helicopter blades, I dare not speak
My fear that spring will not so much postpone

Itself as be junked for good. Reproving me,
Pale daffodils blow mute challenge through the rain;
And, deft as a spoofing conjurer, pulling tricks
Off after mock-disaster, once again
Sun kindles green fire from tree to tree to tree.

IX
May

It becomes summer I heard the landlord say

In German, that May eight years back
As he bulked by the open door against jet-chalked blue
Noonday sky and the white effervescence of black-
Thorn bloom. *Es wird Sommer.* A foreign bug
Skimmed, windborne, through the cool still-shadowed pub.

Summer becoming a place, a time of day:

Wind flannelling cheeks as I ride
My bike along deserted afternoons, one free
Hand trailing in lukewarm air; the greentiger glide
Of reflected riverlight on willow leaves
At teatime; bumbling duckling, plump as bees.

News unbecoming summer. I sense decay

Like a rancid mouthwash, a pain
In the liver. I gag over sunwarmed market reeks
Of cod, refried fat, as the hot wind from Ukraine
Shrivels my thoughts to: *critical, dustcloud, core,*
Meltdown – an abracadabra of fear.

Summer encompassed by town: an alleyway

Of starved weeds in a waste of brick:
Littered skips, chock-a-block with Saharafuls of dust
And rubble. My temperature rockets; I fall sick
With an unknown virus – delirious, I search
My atlas for those silent deserts which

May soon become all there is of summer. May

Contracts to a handful of dark
Leaves scratching my invalid window. I re-emerge
To a hugeness of green; stroll, quickening, through the park
Not across it. Horsechestnut leaves are splayed
Beneath a pomp of candles. Every day

Fresh openings. Summer come into full array.

X
June

June hangs fire: cloud billowing thick
And damp, like smoke from hedge-cuttings, obscures
The sun. I budge our swollen, stuck
Front door ajar one morning; through the trick-
Trickle of rain on a garden greenly lush
As fresh-washed salad, bid the cat indoors.

No answering mew and leap. She preys
All morning through my thoughts. That afternoon,
Some instinct walks me to her corpse
Humped by the kerb: dulled fur, a slitted gaze
Above a wildcat snarl. We bury her close
By birds she murdered, kittens that so soon

Relinquished life. The new-made past
Interred, I turn indoors again, unearth
Stratified relics in the teetering, vast
Disorder of our junkroom as I prepare
To ready it against the baby's birth.

Love-letters from my ex-wife, dry
As documents. I marvel at the thin
Charade we made of marriage – soft
And innocently cruel kittens – sigh,
Shrug off ghosts, and post the episode inside
The booming huge communal rubbish bin.

This once, I am inside the skin
That moment provides. Sun, beaconing from clear
Blue, floods into the sharp white box
Of finished room. Paint-streaked, I grin
At kids clowning in the yard, at Maggie, plush
As a ripening peach, July's fulfilment near.

XI
July

The stroke of ten. Huge, pink-white hollyhocks
Nod from the railings of St Pancras' Parish
Church, as my bus rolls by – the ringing clock's

Affirmation echoing mine. This ride
So different from . . . two nights back was it? Garish
Boiled-sweet stoplights, ruthless lorries, false
Trails down angling one-way streets. Inside

The hospital, our restless, whispering wait
For the midwife in a cubicle. Re-reading
Posters, taking nothing in. The late

Hour indicated by the clock at odds
With wakefulness. The midwife, gently kneading
Maggie's overripe belly, thinks the head
Hasn't engaged. A neutral doctor prods,

Agrees, ordains a drip. A snarl of leads
Hooks her to the machine. *When will sensation*
Become pain? she jokes. The folding printout reads

Like a crazy sketch of mesas, alps and spires,
Tracing pain that she sings in incantation:
Come child, come. I talk her through the hours
To a silent plateau. Raucous cockney choirs

Of starlings at dawn . . . my hot, unspoken fears . . .
Time is a nonsense. Sudden strangers, yelling
PUSH. A flattened, purple head appears

In startling alien profile, and our boy
Is crying his fill. I rock him later, telling
His name over like a charm: John Patrick. Mild
Ageless blue eyes explore my features. Joy

Then – and now, as I hurry to him – wild
Voices inside my head that match the swelling
Chimes of St Pancras': *Joy, give you joy of your child.*

XII
August

Eighth month of the year, the dictionary's bald
Statement. In my schoolboy's book, a splendid
Unwritten chapter, crowning all those scrawled,
Red-annotated pages. August ended
Eleven drudging months – the only one
Unmarked by education – reconnecting
My self to myth. Stroked mindless by the sun,
I'd chase it over sand-dunes, half-expecting
An end to all skylines, where it hung suspended

Eternally. The flawless, long perspective
Back to childhood is an artist's trick, deceptive,

As mine was then. *August: a circus clown*
Of the maladroit type – the one whose belt and braces
Won't keep his checkered bags from shooting down
To a trombone fart. How memory effaces
Those holiday letdowns; like the windblown sand
Burying condoms, dropped ice-lollies, broken
Spades and glass. Car breakdowns scotching planned
Outings; last waves through rain; those dismal token
Smiles, plastered by gales to cold-contorted faces

Skulking by windbreaks – though I tried averting
Such shocks by anticipation, they kept hurting.

August: majestic, venerable, sublime –
An ancient head in stone. I sit, contented
By my sleeping son on a village lawn; sense time
Still as a sundial, clearcut as the scented
Blocks of privet. Even the well-kept grass
And gravel throw long shadows in this brazing,
Eight o'clock evening light that floats a mass
Of cumulus. An instant without gazing
Back or forward – loss, desire both circumvented.

XIII
September

Horsechestnuts crushed on the road. My tiny son,
So lately born, dies in his pram – like that –
At a Harvest Supper. At home, alone,
I cradle the phone on Maggie's camouflaged
Message of death; reach hospital to learn
What I know already. We cling together, one
In grief. John's nodding body, limp
As a newborn's, cool flesh a bloodless tone
Of ivory. We kiss the pursed mouth, turn
Into a life as horizonless and flat

As an icefield. Despair is a shambling thing
In down-at-heel slippers, in a maze
Of corridors; an idiot lurching beast,
Steered at the elbow by friends from room to room:
Coroner, registrar – scrawling its dumb
Name to a typewriter's clatter; encountering
Joy's mirror image at each turn.
The death certificate is signed. Released
From red-tape, we rethread our route in numb
Silence, down echoing antiseptic ways

To autumn's hanging damp. A pride of slack
Giraffe-necked planetrees, arched in from the walls
Of the hospital courtyard, interweaves
Its variegating canopy above
A fountain-speckled pool that brims the stone
Lip of its basin. Locked in a desert of black
Asphalt mottled with the green
Litter of prematurely scattered leaves;
Discoursing through the motions of its own
Self-contained cycle – it gathers, rises, falls.

About the Author

COLIN ROWBOTHAM was born in Manchester in 1949. Since 1972, he has lived and worked in inner London; apart from a year teaching in a Gymnasium in West Germany, 1977-78. He has taught infants and juniors, ESL with Pakistanis and Bangladeshis, Adult Literacy, and worked for four years in a co-operative teaching English as a foreign language. At present he works in Hackney tutoring teenagers who have been expelled from mainstream education. He is a keen fencer.

About the Artist

STEPHEN PICKLES, who has designed a number of recent covers for Littlewood, read English at York University at the same time as Colin Rowbotham, and then went on to take a further degree, this time in Fine Arts at Hull College of Higher Education. He is a part-time teacher in further and adult education, and a retained fireman at Mytholmroyd. He has exhibited in many mixed shows in the North of England, and in 1986 had a one-man show at Rochdale, and in 1987 took part in a two-person show at Halifax.